In the North Western world love is expressed in different ways and comes at you like a train at full speed. Passionate about writing, between adjusting in the U.S putting medical school on pause, aim for nursing school and a broken union; James started writing again about this beautiful thing called love, in fact, who does not dream of what we call "the perfect life" having a person in whom we can confide, have fun, and indulge with no holding back? Indeed, his primary concern since this is his 3rd work: is to present poetry as an art accessible to all, that everyone can enjoy reading, so he wrote this book and made sure the texts are simple, rich, easy to relate and read, very revolting, playful, and academic, so that the readers themselves would want to take up their pen in turn to write their own story, and get better at loving their partner because sometimes we get stranded in the sea of love and get blind by the past however when reality kicks in….

"Special thanks to: Caijee Jaysen M., Maryse, Rodney, Jean Wood Julien, Raymond Julien, James Ophin, Fremiaud Myrthil, Trecy JL, Jacques Myrthil, Sherley, Oluitch, Jennifer F., Jamesha C., Katiusquie Pierre, Oscar and Lyly."

"Love is a tyrant which **spares no one."**

Pierre Corneille, "The Cid" (1637).

Introduction

This story is a story of a literature teacher that has one last show before his retirement. He then invited three longtime friends to come to the show. But shortly after the show the unexpected happened.

CHAPTER I

LULLABY

Have you ever found yourself pondering over the future and questioning the impact of certain decisions? It is not uncommon to experience doubt when faced with situations that seem incongruous with past experiences. Consider this scenario: a woman who once loved you wholeheartedly, accepted your engagement request and subsequently agreed to marriage. However, now she seems determined to discard everything you both painstakingly built together. The notion of this drastic change may seem impossible to fathom. How could the love of your life suddenly love you out of pity? Naturally, you find yourself yearning for answers, seeking to understand the reason behind such a perplexing shift in emotions. In order to unravel this enigma, it is crucial to delve deeper into the complexities of human emotions and the intricate dynamics of relationships. Love, though often described as an eternal and unwavering force, is subject to the ebbs and flows of life. As time progresses, individuals evolve and transform, and with these changes, their feelings and priorities can undergo significant shifts. It is important to acknowledge that love, while powerful, is not immune to external factors that may influence its course. Life's challenges, unforeseen circumstances, and personal growth can all contribute to altering the dynamics of a relationship. Perhaps your partner's decision is rooted in a desire for personal fulfillment, a need to explore new horizons, or an unforeseen change in priorities. These factors, which may seem perplexing and even hurtful, are not uncommon in the intricate tapestry of human connections. While it may be disheartening to witness the dissolution of a once cherished bond, it is essential to remember that love is a complex emotion that cannot be reduced to a single reason or explanation. Instead of dwelling solely on the doubt and confusion that this situation evokes, it may be beneficial to focus on personal growth and self-reflection. By embracing the uncertainty and allowing oneself to heal, new opportunities for love and happiness may emerge in unexpected ways.

CHAPTER II

IN THE REALM OF LOVE

In the realm of love, a vast and intricate landscape unravels before us. It is a terrain where passion and vulnerability intertwine, where joy and anguish dance in an eternal embrace. Love is a journey that takes us through exhilarating highs and devastating lows, where the heart knows both boundless ecstasy and profound sorrow. In this intricate tapestry of emotions, suffering becomes an inherent part of the equation.

It is a highly, well-adjusted and a one sided paradoxical phenomenon, where one may believe they have found contentment, only to realize that beneath the surface, a lingering sense of unease persists. It is the fear of losing what one holds most dear, a fear that gnaws at the soul with an almost imperceptible intensity. This suffering, however, is unlike any other. It is a pain that leaves no visible wounds, yet its presence is palpable. It is a real and sharp pain that defies every if not all conventional understanding, for it is both benign and gentle, yet searing and relentless. It is a pain that resides not in the physical realm, but within the depths of the heart and mind, an ache that resonates through every fiber of our being. And yet, despite the inherent suffering that love entails, we continue to embark on this perilous journey time and time again. Perhaps it is because, deep within our souls, we recognize that love holds the key to a future that is brimming with hope and possibility.

It is the belief that within the realms of love. We can discover a profound connection that transcends the boundaries of time and space. As we navigate the uncharted waters of love, we tread upon the path that has been trodden by countless souls before us. We are driven by the relentless optimism that the future holds the promise of a love that is both enduring and transformative. And it is this unwavering faith in the power of love that sustains us through the inevitable tribulations and heartaches that lie in wait. So, as we navigate the labyrinthine corridors of love, let us remember that suffering is an integral part of the journey. It is through our capacity to endure and transcend this suffering that we pave the way for a future that is imbued with the richness and depth that only love can bestow. May we embrace the pain, for it is through the crucible of suffering that our hearts are forged, and our love is made stronger.

In contemplating the essence of our existence, it becomes evident that happiness and suffering are if not the only fundamental threads that weave the tapestry of our lives. These contrasting emotions, like two sides of a coin, serve as poignant reminders that we are truly alive, experiencing the spectrum of human emotions. Imagine a world devoid of love, devoid of hatred, devoid of sorrow and weeping. Would such a life truly be living? It is through love that we find solace, connection, and the profound ability to touch the depths of our souls. It is through hatred that we understand the power of our convictions, the strength of our values, and the importance of standing up for what we believe in. And it is through sorrow and weeping that we acknowledge the vulnerability of our hearts, the fragility of our existence, and the capacity for growth and transformation. As I sat by her side, watching her slumber peacefully, I couldn't help but marvel at the symphony of life that unfolded before me. Her rhythmic breathing resonated like a melodic composition, akin to a full episode of a classic musical. Each note, so delicately orchestrated, could only be discerned by the most discerning musicians. It was a pure symphony of existence, a testament to the beauty and complexity of life that I found myself endlessly captivated by, never tiring of its enchanting melody. Reflecting on the quality and the love aspect of life, I realized that anything that truly brings forth good can also carry the potential for evil. Love, with all its transformative power, is no exception. Yet, is it not worth the risk of potential pain when we consider the profound meaning it can bestow upon our lives? Love, in all its forms, has the ability to shape us, challenge us, and propel us towards growth and self-discovery. It is in the face of adversity and vulnerability that we find the strength to overcome, to love fiercely and unconditionally. The impact of love, both positive and potentially painful, is a testament to the richness and depth of our human experience. In the grand tapestry of life, where happiness and suffering intermingle, where love and pain dance hand in hand, we find the essence of our existence. It is through these intricate threads that we discover the true meaning of being alive. And in embracing the future, with all its uncertainties and complexities, we recognize that the impact of our choices and experiences shape the very fabric of our lives. So, let us embrace love, let us embrace the risk, and let us find solace in the understanding that it is through these profound emotions that we truly live.

CHAPTER III
TWO SIDED SWORDS

Anything that really does well can do evil, and love too! Do you not think it is worth risking pain when you know that a simple risk can give meaning to your life?

The confusion was finally over, and as clarity washed over me, I found myself immersed in a whirlwind of emotions that were both exhilarating and profound. These sensations were unlike some things or anything I had ever experienced before, taking me on a rollercoaster ride through the depths of my soul. My heart thumped with a fervor that matched the intensity of my newfound emotions, each beat echoing the future impact they would have on my life. It was as if a dormant fire had been sparked within me, igniting a passion that radiated through every fiber of my being. A wave of heat surged through my body, causing my skin to flush with a warmth that mirrored the intensity of my feelings. But amidst this fiery fervor, there was a subtle chill that ran down my spine, a reminder that love, in all its complexities, could also leave us vulnerable. Tremors coursed through me, a physical manifestation of the emotional earthquake that had taken hold of my soul. It was a bittersweet sensation, for while I reveled in the ecstasy of love's embrace, I also feared the day when these sensations might fade away. The thought of losing this connection, this intoxicating torture of emotions, was enough to send shivers down my spine. In the midst of this turmoil, I realized that I had never felt more alive than in that very moment. Love had transformed me, awakening a part of myself that I never knew existed. It had opened my eyes to the beauty and fragility of the human experience, reminding me that life's most profound moments often come hand-in-hand with pain and vulnerability. As I stood on the precipice of this newfound love, I knew that the journey ahead would be filled with challenges and uncertainties. But I also knew that the impact it would have on my future was undeniable. Love had the power to shape and redefine who we are, to push us beyond our limits, and to show us the true depths of our hearts. And so, I embraced these complex sensations, treasuring each moment of joy, pain, and everything in between. For it was in this beautiful chaos that I found the essence of what it truly means to be alive, to experience the transformative power of love.

In the tumultuous aftermath of heartbreak, one is left with more than just sleepless nights and inconsolable tears. It is a state of being that engulfs the soul, leaving behind a landscape reminiscent of post-war ruins. Like a valiant falcon, equipped with a horned and formidable beak, one may tirelessly search for remnants of life within this desolate terrain, but no matter how deep the excavation, no pain can be inflicted. For the heart is already lifeless, devoid of any sensation, sense, breath, or nerve. The broken heart, a metaphorical battlefield strewn with the remnants of lost love, bears witness to the devastating toll of emotional warfare. It is a hallowed ground of shattered dreams and unfulfilled promises, where the echoes of past joys and shared experiences reverberate through the desolate air. In this desolate aftermath, one cannot help but be haunted by the relentless ghosts of remorse and regret. Memories, once cherished, now torment the mind, replaying like a melancholy symphony, each note a painful reminder of what once was. It is a symphony that holds the power to pierce the depths of one's being, stirring a profound ache that resonates with the rhythm of a broken heart. Yet, amidst this heart-wrenching agony, there is a paradoxical numbness that pervades. The pain is so all-encompassing, so consuming, that it renders the heart impervious to further harm. Like an injured soldier who can no longer feel the blows of battle, the broken heart becomes a fortress of emotional detachment, shielded from the outside world. With each passing day, the falcon of time may attempt to chip away at the remains of this wounded heart, hoping to revive its dormant sensitivity. But alas, it is a futile endeavor. The heart, once shattered, cannot be pieced back together. It becomes a relic of the past, forever frozen in a state of emotional suspension. So, we must tread carefully, for those whose hearts bear the scars of love's demise. We must approach with empathy and understanding, for the pain they carry runs deep, like a dormant volcano waiting to erupt. And as we witness their struggle to navigate the treacherous terrain of a broken heart, let us remember that healing takes time, patience, and a gentle touch, for even the most resilient of souls can be shattered by love's cruel hand.

CHAPTER IV

RISE-UP

To truly survive this martyr, one must possess a love that surpasses all boundaries and expectations, for it is love that truly holds the power to transform even the most ordinary existence into an extraordinary adventure. However, let us not forget that every adventure comes at a price, and love is no exception. It demands a costume, a persona, which either toughens your heart like hardened leather or consumes you with an unrelenting obsession for the pursuit of happiness, the pursuit that can elevate you to the pinnacle of bliss, making you the happiest soul on this vast earth. Just like any captivating love story, emotions become the very fabric of this grand narrative. There is the girl, a mysterious enchantress who captures your heart with her mere presence, and there is the man, drawn to her like a moth to a flame. Their souls intertwine, entwined in a dance of joy and sorrow, as destiny weaves its intricate tapestry. There are moments of weeping, where tears cascade down like a gentle rain, cleansing wounds and nurturing the seeds of growth. Yet, through it all, there is an unshakable belief that they are meant to be together, forging an unbreakable bond that defies the odds. But love is not a passive force; it demands effort and commitment from those who dare to embrace its intoxicating allure. It requires unwavering promises, whispered in the darkest of nights, and a resolute will to weather the storms that may threaten their union. Each effort adds a new layer to their story, forming the foundation upon which their love blossoms. It is in these shared efforts that they discover the true essence of love, for it is not merely a fleeting emotion, but a conscious decision to dedicate oneself to another, to stand by their side through thick and thin. In the realm of love, there are no certainties, no guarantees. It is a journey filled with twists and turns, where the destination is never certain. Yet, within the realm of uncertainty lies the beauty of love, for it is in the surrender to its unpredictable nature that true magic is born. It is a dance between two souls, moving in sync to a rhythm only they can hear, creating a symphony of love that resonates deep within their beings. So, as you embark on this martyrdom called love, remember that pain may be an inevitable companion on this path, but it is through this pain that you will discover your truest self. Embrace the challenges, for they are the stepping stones that lead to a love that is steadfast and unyielding. And remember, love is not a destination, but a lifelong journey, an adventure that will forever shape the very core of your existence.

Although love is not a decision, it is a decision to devote yourself to someone.

Well, nevertheless, at a certain age, whether at 7 or 77, you say to yourself, "I have made my decision and I am motivated, in the enthusiasm of the moment, I embark on this adventure and I want it to be serious."

I had always dreamed of living with a companion who is of extraordinary beauty but also of a partner who brings me a meaning, and who adds different and pleasant flavors to my life. What man doesn't dream of it?

And it was then at the age of 21 that I met a rare beauty of Haitian origin, refined, educated, in short, the dream jewel for which I never cease to glow. A smile on her and I melt. I'll do things for her that she never dares to ask me. I imagined walking her and me on the moving sand, hand in hand, enjoying our last cycle of life, with short days and long nights of love, wonderful children and pleasant little children who for the summer were going to come to spend a vacation with their grandparents.

But everything has changed, I now see myself every day, sitting at a table, reading old books by Racine, Baudelaire, Ardouin, Durand etc. Alone and single, not because I wanted to, but rather because love had disappointed me and cast me into forgetfulness.

This is the story of an old and successful writer that does live poetry, and when one night he will shake the world and even his friends.

CHAPTER V

THE CHRONICLE: WHAT MAKES YOU FEEL ALIVE?

"No one can tell me that he has never had a broken heart, not even once, and if there is one, it exists on other forms like aluminum and steel"

In love, we suffer, we are constantly suffering, and we think we are happy but we are suffering. We suffer from the fear of losing what we have most dearly, we suffer from pain without wounds, pain without pain but from a benign pain. But in short, happiness and suffering are the only things that remind us that we are alive.

Without love, without hatred, without sorrow, are we even alive?

And this is how began the diary of a young man who fell in love with a girl whose he is 4 years older, they had a life of reverence and 9 months he wanted to marry the girl because he loved so much and wanted to go to something else and take another scale with their relationship but the girl refused, but throughout the relationship a lot of things came up, the girl had a secret diary that the young man had discovered and every day he continued he went to her house and took the newspaper and put it back to his place the next day, but one day the girl's sister discovered the newspaper as well and this diary was talking about the sister, she began to write her pain and pain for 4 years. One month after their dispute, the young man decided to continue his studies in another country, when he returned to Miami, about seven years after a box of mail unopened awaited him, it was the girl, in the box there was the newspaper well enveloped, on the street she carried a smile in her face all day but a smile that ended when she put her foot on the threshold of the door of her house. She then decided to return to the "US Army" and during an ambush in Baghdad She got a bullet at the chest level and couldn't survive, in her equipment we found a newspaper in which a name and an address are written, and then we sent the newspaper to the address, he leafleted page by page the newspaper and warm tears flowed on his face, he kept the journal throughout his life and forgetting the girl became almost impossible.

As the years passed, the weight of age settled upon him, each passing day etching new lines of experience upon his face. In a society that often placed value on societal norms and expectations, he found himself becoming a target of critical judgment and the object of ridicule among his friends. They couldn't help but question his love life, pondering what he could have possibly done during his prime years of 20-22 and 40-45. The curiosity lingered, leaving him exposed to the pain of their probing inquiries. Yet, their questioning didn't cease there. They delved deeper, wondering why he hadn't taken the traditional path of marriage and fatherhood. They couldn't comprehend how he had managed to remain childless, when others his age had already embraced the joys of parenthood. Their judgmental gazes bore into his soul, leaving him to question himself and his choices. The truth was, his journey had been far from conventional. His younger years, the formative 17-19s, had been filled with a different kind of growth and self-discovery. While his peers sought companionship and settled down, he had embarked on a path of self-reflection and personal development. It was a time when he had explored the depths of his own soul, nurtured his passions, and honed his skills. He had chosen to prioritize his own growth and happiness over conforming to societal expectations. As for the idea of adopting children, it wasn't a decision he took lightly. He believed that bringing a child into this world was a responsibility that required careful consideration. He understood the immense weight of nurturing and guiding another human being, and he believed that he had to be in the right place emotionally, mentally, and financially to embark on such a journey. It wasn't a choice he would make simply to appease others' expectations; instead, he wanted to ensure that he could provide a stable and loving environment for a child to thrive. The pain of being judged for his unconventional path was undeniable, but he held onto the belief that his choices were valid and meaningful. He knew that societal norms shouldn't define one's worth or happiness.

Instead, he had chosen to forge his own path, to prioritize his personal growth and fulfillment, and to embrace the freedom that comes with being true to oneself.

Every single day, he found himself trapped in excruciating situations that not only tested his endurance but also left him feeling utterly unsettled. It was as if the universe conspired to put him in judgmental and painful circumstances, one after another, with no respite in sight. However, a glimmer of solace would seep through the cracks of his distress when he reached into the depths of his blouse, retrieving a bundle of aged sheets of paper. These seemingly unassuming leaves held an extraordinary power: they were the only entities, apart from himself, that bore witness to the old man's deepest secrets. In fact, they were a testament to his clandestine existence, a carefully penned manuscript that he had authored but had never been able to share with the world. This collection of memories, his intimate diary, was a chronicle that unraveled the enigmatic chapters of his twenties and early thirties, recounting his life's journey, the heart-wrenching tale of a refused engagement, and the countless injustices he had endured in the name of love. With each turn of a page, the old man's emotions materialized in vivid detail, his words etching a painful yet poignant portrait of a life marred by heartache and disappointment. The weight of his unspoken sorrows was lifted ever so slightly as he entrusted his innermost thoughts to these delicate sheets of paper, knowing that they held the power to preserve his legacy, even if it remained hidden from the eyes of the world. As he navigated through the turbulent currents of existence, these pages served as his silent confidants, offering solace and companionship in a world that often felt harsh and unforgiving. They became his refuge, a sanctuary where he could unabashedly pour out his soul, unburdening himself from the judgmental gaze of society. And though the pain of his experiences still lingered, it was through his words that he found solace, transforming his suffering into a poignant narrative that resonated with the deepest corners of his being. In the quiet moments, when the weight of the world pressed heavily upon his shoulders, he would unfurl these precious papers and allow his fingers to trace the faded ink, reliving the emotions captured within. They were a testament to his resilience, a tangible reminder that despite the hardships and the relentless judgment of others, his story was worth telling. And as he continued to face the challenges that life threw his way, he found solace in knowing that his truth, his pain, and his triumphs were forever etched upon those fragile sheets of paper. Without any introduction or preface, he presented his chronicle in a narrative of about 45 pages, written in black and dark ink.

The young man lived in the United States, his mother, father and sister had remained in the Caribbean. Living alone, far from his family, He had to face many adventures, of which Love was the most stubborn and the hardest to overcome however the only break up, and separation that hurts him the most was the separation of him and his wife based on other people's view and beliefs and this pain could never end.

The show was filled with stories but mainly focus on love, however three of his friends that attended the event were approached by his apprentice and were given a journal.

CHAPTER VI

THE CHRONICLE: DIARY OF AN OLD MAN

It was an extraordinary moment when our paths crossed once again, marking our second face-to-face encounter. The sheer serendipity of it all took my breath away, just as it had during our initial meeting. My heart, seemingly synchronized with the rhythm of the universe, pounded with an intensity that spoke volumes about the impact she had on me. Since that memorable day in March, our conversations had ceased, leaving a void that could only be filled by the warmth of her presence. And now, here we were, standing before each other, ready to embark on a new chapter of our connection. As she spoke, her voice resonated with a melody that seemed to carry the promise of a future filled with endless possibilities. Her smile, radiant as ever, illuminated the room and cast a spell on my weary soul. In that instant, it was as if time stood still, and all that mattered was the sheer joy of being in her presence. It was a smile that breathed life into my being, igniting a spark of hope and excitement deep within. As our brief embrace ended, I couldn't help but inquire about her well-being, delving into the intricacies of her life. I asked about her parents, eager to know how they were faring in an ever-changing world. Curiosity piqued, I inquired about her studies, curious to learn how she was shaping her future amidst the challenges and opportunities that lay ahead. Inquisitive by nature, I sought to uncover the intricacies of her social life, wondering how she navigated the complexities of friendships and connections in a rapidly evolving society. And, of course, I couldn't resist inquiring about her family, the cornerstone of her existence, eager to understand how they shaped her values and aspirations. Our conversation, though brief, was filled with a sense of anticipation for what the future held. With each word exchanged, it became apparent that our reunion would have a profound impact on both our lives, propelling us forward on a shared journey of growth and discovery. Little did we know that this unexpected encounter would serve as a catalyst, setting in motion a series of events that would shape the course of our lives. The future, once uncertain, now shimmered with the possibility of something extraordinary, something that would forever alter the trajectory of our intertwined destinies.

Our discussion, though brief, was a truly delightful encounter that left a lasting impression. As we caught up, I couldn't help but notice how unchanged she was, her radiant smile and impeccable teeth as captivating as ever. In the midst of exchanging contact information, an unexpected interruption occurred as her mother made an appearance. Feeling a sudden pang of discomfort, I gracefully excused myself and left. However, even as I walked away, my thoughts were consumed by her presence. Days turned into weeks, and I found myself constantly reminiscing about our encounter. It was on a serene evening, a mere night after her birthday, about two months after our paths had crossed once again, that a message from her illuminated my screen. She summoned me to her side, urging me to come and retrieve her. Intrigued by the mysterious nature of her request, we both harboring an insatiable curiosity, we agreed to meet once more. Little did we know that this decision would shape our future in ways we could never have anticipated. The impact of that fateful meeting would set the stage for a journey filled with unforeseen twists and turns

CHAPTER VII

33

A LOVE STORY

At precisely nine o'clock, my heart raced with anticipation as I stood before the barrier, eagerly awaiting his arrival. The moment our eyes met, I couldn't help but be captivated by the radiant glow emanating from his being. Oh, those eyes! They held a depth that seemed to peer into the future, hinting at the profound impact we were about to experience together. As time went on, we discovered an uncanny connection between us. It was as if our souls were intertwined, our expectations aligned in perfect harmony. Our characters, we soon realized, were not just similar but perhaps even identical, complementing each other in the most extraordinary way. Without each other, our lives felt incomplete, as if a vital piece was missing. Days turned into weeks, and weeks into months, as we found solace in each other's company. Every day, we eagerly looked forward to our time spent together, cherishing each shared moment as if it were a precious gem. Love, once a mere concept to me, had transformed into something tangible, something that enveloped my entire being. This newfound love, like a drawer full of mysteries, pushed me to question myself and explore the depths of my own being. It encouraged introspection and self-discovery, as if the mere presence of this extraordinary connection opened doors I never knew existed. It was a love that not only brought joy and fulfillment but also challenged me to grow and evolve as an individual. In this journey of love, we couldn't help but ponder the future and the impact it would have on us. Would our connection withstand the test of time? How would it shape our lives? These questions lingered in the back of our minds, adding an element of excitement and anticipation to our shared journey. As we embraced the present, we were aware that the future held endless possibilities. The impact of our love, we believed, would ripple through our lives, leaving an indelible mark on our hearts and souls. With each passing day, our bond grew stronger, and our love became a beacon of hope, guiding us towards a future that promised endless adventures and boundless love. So, hand in hand, we ventured into the unknown, ready to face whatever challenges and joys the future had in store for us. Together, we would create a story that would leave an everlasting imprint on our lives and the lives of those around us.

When we're together, she exudes a warmth that envelops me in a cocoon of affectionate gestures. Her generosity knows no bounds as she lavishes me with caresses that leave an indelible mark on my heart. Each moment we spend side by side becomes an opportunity for her to showcase her unwavering love and tenderness. Whether we're strolling hand in hand down the bustling streets of the city or taking a leisurely walk in the park, she never fails to let me grasp her delicate hand, intertwining our fingers like a promise of a future filled with shared adventures. Inside the sanctuary of my home, our connection grows even stronger. As we gather around the dining table, her foot discreetly finds its way to mine, a subtle yet powerful symbol of our unity. In the dimly lit cinema, the proximity of our legs creates an electric current, igniting a spark of anticipation and excitement. And when we lounge on the sofa, she willingly rests her head upon my chest, allowing me the pleasure of serving as her comforting pillow, a sanctuary she seeks in my embrace. Even in moments of retreat, she finds a way to express her affection. As she pulls away from our intimate closeness, her hand tenderly brushes against mine, leaving behind a lingering sensation of her love. It's in these small yet significant gestures that I realize the profound impact she has on my life. With every caress, every touch, and every kiss, she reshapes my future, molding it into a tapestry woven with love, trust, and unwavering devotion. In her gentle touch lies the promise of a future where our love continues to blossom, where our souls remain intertwined, and where the impact of her affection resonates in every corner of our lives. Together, we navigate the intricacies of love, creating a symphony of emotions that dances to the rhythm of our hearts. And as we journey through life hand in hand, her generous caresses serve as a constant reminder that true love is both a gift and a privilege, one that I cherish with every fiber of my being.

CHAPTER VIII

Love is an emotion that transcends mere heartbeats; it encompasses a world of extraordinary experiences and profound connections. From the exhilarating first date filled with nervous anticipation, to the heartfelt promises that bind two souls together, love has the power to shape our lives in ways we never thought possible. It is a force that not only brings individuals closer but also has the potential to impact the future of our world. Imagine a future where love is not just a fleeting emotion, but a guiding principle that shapes our choices and actions. In this vision of the future, love is not limited to romantic relationships alone; it extends to encompass a love for humanity, the environment, and everything that surrounds us. When we think of love, we often associate it with the purity and innocence of a blossoming relationship. It is in this state of love's infancy that we find a pristine and paradisiacal environment. Love has the power to create a world untainted by the chaos and negativity that often plague our society. It is a force that has the potential to transform our surroundings into a sanctuary of tranquility and harmony. The impact of love reaches far beyond the individuals involved. It has the power to inspire and influence the actions of those around us. Love is contagious, spreading its warmth and positivity to everyone it touches. It is through love that we can build a future where compassion and empathy prevail, where acts of kindness become the norm rather than the exception. Think back to the moments when love has touched your life. Whether it was a single instance or a multitude of experiences, the impact of love is undeniable. It is in these moments that we truly understand the depth and significance of this extraordinary emotion. Love has the ability to transform us, to bring out the best version of ourselves, and to ignite a fire within us that propels us towards a brighter future. So, let us embrace love in all its forms and cherish the profound impact it has on our lives. Let us strive to create a future where love reigns supreme, where its power and influence shape not only our personal relationships but also the world we inhabit. For it is in love that we find the key to unlocking a future filled with boundless possibilities and endless joy.

CHAPTER IX

DELUSIONAL ILLUSIONS

Love is a transcendent force that goes far beyond the mere beat of a heart. It encompasses the profound experiences of a first date, the heartfelt promises made, and the transformative power of a love that is both wholesome and enduring. It creates a world so pristine and idyllic, where nothing exists except the purity of its essence. She was the embodiment of all his dreams, and he, in turn, fulfilled her every wish. These emotions, etched in our hearts, remain vivid no matter how many times we have experienced them. They shape our future and leave an indelible impact on our lives.

Love is not simply a rhythmic heartbeat; it transcends the confines of a physical sensation. It blooms, like a fragile flower, with every first date and blossoms with the exchange of promises that hold the key to a future filled with hope. This love, untainted and everlasting, creates a sanctuary of serenity, where every corner is adorned with the grace of a paradise untarnished by imperfections. Without her, nothing existed; she was the very embodiment of his dreams, and he was the fulfillment of all her desires. How can one forget the overwhelming tide of emotions that washes over the heart, leaving an indelible mark, imprinted with the power to transform lives? It is a force that touches us once, twice, or countless times, forever shaping our future and impacting the very essence of our being.

CHAPTER X

WHAT IS LOVE?

Love is a force that transcends time and space, shaping our future and leaving an indelible impact on our lives. It manifests itself in myriad ways, influencing our behaviors and ways of proceeding, whether in the presence or absence of our beloved. When love takes hold of our hearts, we become consumed by its power and everything else pales in comparison. The first kiss, that electrifying moment when our lips meet, becomes etched in our memories, forever marking the beginning of a journey filled with passion and devotion. The first caress, a tender touch that ignites a flame within us, becomes a symbol of the deep connection we share. As the night unfolds, we find solace in each other's arms, basking in the warmth and intimacy that love brings. In those moments, we feel invincible, believing that together we can conquer the world and make a lasting impact on society. But what exactly is love? It is a complex and multifaceted emotion that defies easy definition. Love is the unbreakable bond that ties two souls together, inspiring acts of kindness, compassion, and selflessness. It is the driving force behind our desire to protect and nurture those we hold dear. In the future, love will continue to shape our world, influencing our decisions and actions. Its impact will be felt not only in our personal relationships but also in the broader scope of society. Love has the power to bridge divides, heal wounds, and unite communities.

It inspires us to strive for a better world, where empathy and understanding prevail.

In our ever-evolving world, the future holds countless possibilities, shaping our lives and leaving a lasting impact on our existence. One such phenomenon that has stood the test of time is the intense and pleasant feeling that encourages beings to unite. It is a force that transcends boundaries, cultures, and languages, creating a perfect balance known as the body-to-body connection. This union of hearts, though often celebrated as a metaphysical experience, is not devoid of its scientific underpinnings. When two individuals come together, a chemistry unlike any other unfolds. It is a delicate dance of neurotransmitters, hormones, and synapses firing in perfect harmony. This intricate blend of science and emotion is what drives our desire, our appetite for connection. Yet, as much as we yearn for this passionate thirst to be quenched, reality has a way of tempering our expectations. The future, with all its promises, can sometimes cast a shadow on the present.

While the initial moments of unity may be filled with happiness and joy, there is always the realization that not everything is as fabulous as one would expect. As time passes, the memory of that initial connection can leave a sour taste, like a bittersweet flavor that lingers long after the moment has passed. But perhaps, it is this very contrast that makes these connections so profound. The impact they have on our lives, despite their fleeting nature, is a testament to the depth of human emotion. It reminds us that even in the face of imperfection, the pursuit of unity and the yearning for a genuine connection is what makes us truly alive. So, as we navigate the uncharted territories of the future, let us cherish these moments of intense connection. Let us revel in the chemistry that binds us together and appreciate the metaphysical forces at play. For in the tapestry of life, it is these connections that weave the most vibrant and unforgettable threads, leaving an indelible mark on our hearts and souls.

CHAPTER XI

THE PERFECT MATCH

Her body, with its perfect curves and breathtaking symmetry, is a testament to the beauty of human anatomy. From the roundness of her breasts that seem sculpted by a master artist's hand, to the elegant shape of her body that effortlessly captivates the eye, she is a true masterpiece of high-level architecture. Even the triangular figure that forms her lower abdomen adds a touch of allure, a subtle hint of sensuality that leaves one spellbound. In the intimate moments shared between us, a world of ecstasy unfolds. With every touch, every caress, the future impact of our connection is felt deep within our souls. The chemistry between our bodies ignites a passion that transcends physical pleasure, reaching a level of intimacy that words fail to capture. As our bodies intertwine, the future implications of this profound connection become clear. It is not merely a fleeting moment of pleasure, but a profound experience that leaves an indelible mark on our hearts and minds. With each embrace, we are building a foundation of trust, respect, and understanding that will shape our future together. The impact of our union extends far beyond the confines of the bedroom. It is a catalyst for personal growth, a catalyst that pushes us to explore the depths of our desires, and to embrace vulnerability with open arms. Our intimate encounters serve as a reminder that we are not just physical beings, but emotional and spiritual creatures yearning for connection and transcendence. In the grand tapestry of life, moments like these hold the power to shape our destinies. They remind us of the immense potential we possess to create a future filled with love, passion, and deep fulfillment. As we surrender to the pleasure that courses through our veins, we are propelled forward into a future where our shared experiences become the foundation for a bond that withstands the test of time. So, let us revel in the exquisite beauty of our physical connection, knowing that it is not just a momentary pleasure, but a catalyst for a future filled with love, growth, and the profound impact of two souls intertwined

In a world where skepticism often prevails, it's easy to dismiss the notion of pure and eternal love as a mere myth perpetuated by fools. Many consider it a joke, a fable, or a fairy tale. After all, only fools would dare to believe otherwise, right? Love, it seems, is nothing more than a figment of our imaginations. However, let us not brush aside the impact that love has on our lives, both now and in the future. As humans, we are driven by a relentless pursuit of happiness, and love, without a doubt, plays a pivotal role in this quest. It is through love that we find solace, comfort, and a sense of belonging. Without it, life can feel like a dark abyss, filled with uncertainty and unease. It is true that love can be fragile and fleeting. Yet, it is precisely this impermanence that makes it all the more precious. Like a delicate flower, love requires nurturing, care, and attention to flourish. And while some may argue that jokes and fables have an ephemeral existence, love, in its essence, transcends time and space. Think about the impact of love on individuals and society as a whole. Love has the power to heal wounds, bridge divides, and inspire greatness. It has the ability to bring out the best in us, igniting a fire within our souls that propels us forward. Love gives us the strength to overcome obstacles and face adversity head-on. While love may not always last in the way we envision it, its effects ripple through our lives, shaping our experiences and molding our character. It leaves an indelible mark on our hearts, reminding us that we are capable of experiencing profound connections with others. So, yes, love may be a subject that is often intertwined with jokes and fables. But let us not be quick to dismiss its significance. For in a world that can often feel cold and unforgiving, love offers warmth, compassion, and a sense of purpose. It is a force that transcends the boundaries of time and space, leaving an everlasting impact on our lives

CHAPTER XII
CHAOS

Pure and eternal love is nothing more than a myth of fools, a joke, fables, fairy tales, and fools are those who dare to believe otherwise, love itself is only fables. I cannot also ignore that every man on this earth is in search of what is called happiness, and except for love offers what is known as true love, without love you are nothing but horror, you feel uncomfortable, and it is good to know that you are loved, but love is fragile and does not last, jokes, do they last? Do fables last? However yes love exists but not pure and eternal. Everyone knows different stories but we cannot ignore that love hurts and really hurts, but we live to love and it will never stop, it is our meeting point on the axes of life.

Time was passing slowly, each day is an adventure, a beautiful one that we both could not have enough of. We do everything together, we even finish each other's sentences because we were in complete harmony. But chaos!

When religion surfaced

Religion has always been arguably one of the pillars of the fundamental aspects of all human society for hundreds of centuries, serving individuals as a compass, acting as repositories of moral guidance and a link to something greater than themselves. However, the role of religion in modern society has become increasingly controversial. While some argue that religion promotes peace, morality and community cohesion, others argue that it perpetuates ignorance, intolerance and division.

One of the main arguments in favor of religion is its ability to provide individuals with a moral compass. Religious teachings often emphasize values such as compassion, forgiveness and honesty. These principles can guide believers in making ethical decisions and contribute to the general well-being of society. In addition, religious communities provide support networks that promote social cohesion and provide individuals with a sense of belonging.

In other cases, critics argue that religion can be used as a facilitating tool or shortcut to try to justify acts of discrimination and violence against certain groups, such as 7th Adventist, Muslims etc. History is filled with examples of religious conflicts leading to wars and persecutions. Additionally, religious dogma can hinder scientific progress by promoting beliefs that contradict empirical evidence.

While religion has undoubtedly played an important role and is an influential agent in the positive formation of human civilization throughout history by providing moral guidance and fostering community cohesion; it is also essential to recognize its potential negative consequences. It is crucial that individuals critically examine their beliefs and ensure that they are not using religion as an excuse for intolerance or ignorance and burying a people or a youth in the dark, or at least used to command, direct and even manipulate people. And finally, the impact of religion on society depends on how society perceives and practices it.

Laying down in the bathtub, I half-opened the tap and was ready for the night, having only one hope that this love would return and that we both would not make the same mistakes again. I am sure that one day I will be able to smile like before but not to love in the same way, I should let her go, leave just like I had done a year after that and who knows, maybe one day we will see each other again in the like way, and as the "melancholy of the century" my life was just swallowed into a black vault that has no way out.

And during the show, with many skills he was talking about what he went through in life, and some answers that people that knew him has been asking him in his whole life were answered in a beautiful poetry motion.

CHAPTER XIII
A MAN SILENT IS NOT A SILENT MAN

In the intricate tapestry of marriage, it is imperative for women to grasp the profound significance behind the silence of their partner. The unspoken words, the pregnant pauses, and the quiet contemplation of a man hold a multitude of hidden meanings, often shaping the very foundation of their relationship. While it may seem enigmatic at first, delving into the depths of this silence can unlock a world of understanding and pave the way for a harmonious future together. The impact of a man's silence in a marriage cannot be overstated. In a society where communication is often hailed as the cornerstone of any successful union, the absence of words can be perplexing, even disconcerting. Yet, it is within these moments of quiet introspection that a man often seeks solace, attempting to process his thoughts and emotions. Rather than interpreting this silence as a sign of indifference or withdrawal, it is crucial for women to embrace it as an opportunity for personal growth and a gateway to profound connection. By recognizing the significance of a man's silence, women can foster an atmosphere of understanding and empathy within their marriage. It is during these moments of wordless contemplation that a man may be grappling with his own insecurities, aspirations, or even concerns about the future. By allowing him the space to collect his thoughts, women can create an environment that encourages open dialogue, where both partners feel safe to express their deepest fears, dreams, and desires. The impact of a man's silence extends far beyond the realm of communication. It can often serve as a barometer for the overall health of a marriage. Just as a calm sea may be a sign of tranquility, a man's silence can indicate a need for introspection or a desire for personal growth. Rather than interpreting this silence as a cause for alarm, it is essential for women to view it as an opportunity for self-reflection and introspection as well. By engaging in personal development, women can strengthen their own emotional well-being and contribute positively to the growth of their marriage.

CHAPTER XIV
LOVE THEORY

Let her go is the only solution, but the evil seems to win if I take this path I will not be able to stop loving her the fire that can't be extinguished; the farther she went away, the more I burned.

In the face of a difficult decision, sometimes the only solution is to let go. However, when it comes to matters of the heart, it can feel like surrendering to evil itself. The impact of such a choice can be profound, leaving one questioning whether they will ever be able to stop loving the person they have had to release. It's as if there is an unquenchable fire burning within, intensifying with each step they take away. The future can seem uncertain when faced with the prospect of letting go. The impact of this decision can ripple through every aspect of life, altering the course of one's journey. But it is in these moments of heartache that we discover the strength within ourselves to endure and overcome. As the flames of love burn relentlessly, one might find solace in knowing that the pain will eventually transform into something new. The future holds the promise of growth and healing, even though it may seem distant and unreachable in the present moment. By embracing the uncertainty of what lies ahead, we open ourselves up to the possibility of new love, new adventures, and new beginnings. It is through this process of letting go that we discover our own resilience, and our ability to rise from the ashes of heartbreak. So, while it may feel like the evil is winning in the immediate aftermath of letting go, remember that the future holds infinite potential. The impact of this difficult decision will be felt, but it is not the end of the story. For as long as the fire burns within, there will always be hope for a brighter tomorrow, where love can be rekindled in unexpected ways.

CHAPTER XV
Fate equal destiny

In certain cultures, the practice of arranged marriage looms large, and it was in this realm of fate that a young man's future was entwined. His heart, brimming with love for a woman he believed to be his soulmate, was shattered when she revealed that her religion forbade her from marrying a Christian. The weight of impact crashed upon him, as he realized that the dream of their union was nothing more than a mirage. His beloved's confession opened the floodgates of doubt, leaving him questioning the authenticity of their connection. It was a remorseful moment, as he discovered that her family had already chosen a suitor, rendering their love story a mere illusion. The truth, like a cruel twist of fate, emerged from the shadows when he inadvertently overheard a conversation between her and her sister. Desperate for answers, he mustered the courage to delve into her personal world, scrolling through her phone, only to find heartbreak waiting for him, he uncovered the dialogue that tore asunder their relationship. Their discussions delved into the intricacies of his religion, casting doubt on its compatibility with her own. The exchanges painted a vivid picture of the obstacles they faced, with her parents even resorting to threats of disownment if she dared to marry him, a Christian. In a world where love and faith intertwine, their story unfolded as a testament to the complexities of cultural traditions. The man grappled with the weight of his shattered dreams, impacted not only by the loss of his beloved but also by the revelation that their love had been tainted by external forces beyond their control. His heart ached with the knowledge that their bond was destined to be nothing more than a fleeting chapter in their lives. He stopped the show and took a moment before thanking the audience for coming

Soon after the show, one of the friends got a call from and old pal and he was devastated learning that the old man killed himself, and called the other friends.

CHAPTER XVI
The end of a man

As the set came to a close, a phone call shattered the air, delivering the devastating news that the elderly man had taken his own life. The impact of this tragic event rippled through the hearts of his three closest friends, leaving an indelible mark of remorse and a profound sense of melancholy. Suddenly, life took on a different hue, and the friends found themselves contemplating their own existence with a newfound depth. With their children now grown and their marriages dissolved, the weight of solitude and uncertainty pressed upon them. Doubt began to cloud their minds as they couldn't help but empathize with the turmoil their departed companion must have faced. The future, once filled with possibilities, now appeared hazy and uncertain, mirroring the inner turmoil they grappled with. As the days turned into weeks, the friends found solace in each other's company, seeking to understand the intricate complexities of life that led their dear friend down such a tragic path. They delved into deep conversations, exploring the profound questions that had plagued humanity for centuries. The impact of their discussions was palpable, as they realized the importance of cherishing every moment, of finding joy amidst the chaos, and of nurturing the relationships that truly mattered. However, despite their efforts to find solace and meaning, the weight of their own battles became unbearable. As they confronted their own demons and the relentless whispers of doubt, each friend, in their own time, succumbed to the darkness that had claimed their dear companion. The echoes of remorse reverberated through the hearts of those who knew them, forever marked by the profound impact their lives had made.

And shortly after each one of these three friends taken over by sadness and darkness, took .their own lives sitting down reading the diary of the old man .

It all started when Sarah started feeling overwhelmed and decide to go see a therapist:

The first session was a very good session but the therapist had something else in mind and things started to get real spicy:

Everything seemed perfect... We see each other almost every day, we spend 5 nights out of 7 together, we call each other.

We even make projects together... Then he keeps telling me he loves me and that I'm the woman of his life.

And yet, a few weeks ago, I had some suspicions and doubts (eh yes, women are very intuitive!), so I decided to read his messages on his mobile. And then, I saw, he went on a date with the girl and went to a hotel, to I knew at a hotel. And that she had reserved a room... in short, I don't make you drawings!!

After reading his message, I confronted him and ran away. Well, he denied everything... and he told me that she was just a friend,

Then, I decided, to believe it, because you know girls, love makes us very happy! And even if I decided to forgive him... in the bottom, I needed to know what was going on in this hotel and to have the heart clean!

So here, I contacted the girl in question by email. Then she told me that this story had hurt her... that she was wrong and that even if he now no longer wants to know anything about her, it has indeed passed between them for several weeks .

He doesn't know that his mistress and I have communicated, and I prefer that he does not know that I have confirmation. But for now, I don't know what to do.

But in the beginning of it all he told me that all his ex-girlfriends cheated on him before he met me and that he never was in a real relationship, That the fact that I got angry with my suspicions a few weeks ago has somehow aroused him and that he will do anything to not lose me...

He's tender and planned, but I'm in trouble. I told him that I don't trust him anymore, that whatever he says, I think it's 99.9% that he lied to me. Then this morning, I got confirmation that it was 100%...

And that's when Sarah and her therapist start to have feelings for each other. He invited her to the bar and throughout the week, they go out every evening and engage in an adventurous and happy and sex-filled life; and without realizing Sarah embarked on two relationships, and she even passed a rule that she and her boyfriend would not have sex without protection; just to punish her a little..

At the end of the year, her boyfriend invited her in a nice and fancy restaurant where he proposed to her over a fancy dinner.

And yes she said yes.

She wanted to stop everything and cut off communications with her therapist just to live her life with her wife.

The wedding was beautiful, but over the course of the days Sarah was not feeling well and showing signs of pregnancy. She went to the hospital and learned she is pregnant but it is impossible the only person she had sex without protection is a therapist and the godly test that she is 6 weeks pregnant. Sarah, having doubts, went to the clinic the next day and had an abortion; for there was probably a 99% chance that the child would not be her husband's child.

Days passed, months passed and their relationship went very well, but everything was going to change when Sarah's sister just stayed with them for a few months and her husband's mother came to stay with them; just to have access to cheaper medical care. Sarah could not handle it; every day it's something. But Sarah has every time mentioned religion as the center of their problems.

And that's when Sarah decides to go to a therapy session with her therapist

Second time

t the beginning Sarah did not want to open up completely but after a good discussion Sarah admits that he has feelings for another man and that she does not know how to do.

then the therapist answers:

Like thousands of people in a couple, you're going through a difficult time with your husband, which has been going on for months, and you've become attracted to someone else.

You do not want to cheat your husband but you want to know the other person better but you feel so guilty!!!

having the two at the same time, is this the ideal route?!

Honestly You are just going through a difficult period of doubts, like many people, what happens to you at this moment can very well happen to him too, you are not an exception to the rule, you have to give yourself a chance, you're by any evidence not happy, it will over time still have an advantage of repercussions on your life of couple, you must face one day or another....

Again a banal story of mother-in-law!

My husband is her 2nd son, the 1st being married and already having a baby of 2 years.

My husband and I have been living together since June and I'd like a baby...

The problem is, I don't know if I can trust him.

I'll explain...

I feel like I'm the only one who sees the future. When I told him that I would like to have a baby, he said yes, but it is always me who proposes his commitments, which he accepts, but I wonder what he thinks.

Besides, I have a boring mother-in-law who is mixed up with everything: she has made many remarks to my poor sister-sister, who is not of the same character as me and lends herself to do.

I wonder if I can trust him because I have the impression that he hasn't cut the cord from his mother: they send each other several mails a day. He tells him everything we're doing or going to do...

I feel like I don't have any privacy!

And when I talk to him about it, he answers that it's me who's the problem and who can't forgive!

Indeed, my mother-in-law once asked me, "If I ever think about it!"

I really like my man but he doesn't see anything abnormal about sending these e-mails every day and does not offer me any solution.

He claims that I want him to break the bridges with his mother as I did with mine... which is wrong because I know better than anyone the cruelty of not having a mother anymore!

I wish he understood it, but any discussion ends with me as a culprit...

By touching her shoulder; the therapist answers her

He's like that and he won't change.

There will be nothing but death that will separate them.

She thinks you and your beautiful sister stole her babies...

She raised them for HER and for herself.

So she didn't make them adults.

And the men staying until their last day as they came out of their mother's skirts to engage in a couple life...

This is a very dark future.

Whatever you say, whatever you do, you'll always be the bad one.

In essence, before the invention of SMS, there was the phone, but it was less discreet... so we had a little more privacy, and tranquility.

In conclusion, he has not cut the cord and he will never cut it because he doesn't even imagine having to.

Nothing prevents you from having a child... but there... that child will be the little son or the little girl of his mother... and that's how he will see the filiation... he only exists through his mother.

And the therapist was so smooth with it he convinced Sarah to go out to dinner Saturday night.

And here was Sarah again embarked on a story with her therapist; after six months she became pregnant, and like all pregnant women she had already felt that the child was not the child of her husband. So she suggested that the therapist take a DNA test during pregnancy. The test that came to the baby is that of the therapist.

The therapist didn't want the child and he was clear on top. Sarah, who had already had an abortion, didn't want a second. She has therefore had the child and throughout the marriage her husband takes care of the child, and the family had never had so much joy.

But something is messing with Sarah, guilt has taken over her and one good evening she started drinking and lost control of the vehicle.

Sarah did not survive the accident leaving a 3-year-old child.

The mourning invaded the family and the husband's life became a nightmare every day he didn't know what to do but he had to be strong for his son.

Conflict of interest

We encounter numerous intriguing individuals who provoke our thoughts and capture our attention. Regardless of gender, it is not uncommon to feel a sense of flattery when someone shows interest in us. However, it is important to refrain from fixating on these fleeting moments and instead engage in open communication with our partners. We should ask ourselves, "What am I doing? I am content with my current relationship, so why jeopardize everything for a temporary pleasure actions.

We can go past any other facts but we have to agree that there are a lot of interesting people out there and sometimes that has our number, and we all have such thoughts, man or woman, and sometimes we find it flattering to be hit on, except that we shouldn't dwell on it and think about it all the time - on the contrary, we should talk to each other and say "what am I doing? I'm happy with my partner, why risk ruining everything for a few minutes of pleasure? And then what happens?

I still have a problem with the expression "cheating on your wife/man".

"Your wife" doesn't belong to you... she may be your "wife", your "companion", because she chose you, but she doesn't belong to you. Her body, her mind, everything is hers. And vice versa. The "husband", the man, also belongs to himself. He's the one who decides whether to be there or not, whether to be attentive or not, whether to be "faithful" or not.

Then, in order to deceive someone, a promise has to be made, and at some point, the promise has to be broken and hidden by a lie. Do you have to promise fidelity to your partner? Well... fidelity, yes, but what kind? A faithful friend is not a single friend for a lifetime. A faithful dog isn't one who lets himself be walked or fed ONLY by his master. So, for there to be deception, clear terms have to be laid down... it's anything but romantic.

And then, when X no longer feels like making love to Y, no longer feels like saying good night, telling her about his day, making her breakfast, should he force himself out of "loyalty"? And Y, if nobody cuddles him/her or makes him/her feel good, does he/she have to stay there and wait "for it to come back"? Is that loyalty?

      The promise is to be faithful to you as long as you're faithful to me and care enough about me that I almost never want to go looking for love, attention, tenderness, a few affectionate gestures from someone else ; who generally needs it as much as I do. Otherwise, even if you didn't go and seduce someone else, but didn't help me when I was sick, didn't take care of me at least a little bit, I'd be the one who'd be cheated. And I'd have a real reason to look elsewhere...

MEN!

In couples, there's a tension between the spirit of Don Juan and the spirit of a son attached to his mother.

This tension creates a kind of male neurosis, which consists on the one hand of the desire to conquer women, all women, but on the other of the sincere desire to take care of his wife and be faithful to her.

This balance gives rise to a form of male insecurity, characterized by an insatiable desire to conquer all women, while also harboring a genuine intent to care for his wife and remain faithful to her. My hypothesis posits that if this tension becomes overwhelming, it can immobilize a man in his commitment to the relationship. Consequently, two detrimental paths emerge: Firstly, there is the passive path, where the man, driven by fear; as bravery must be cultivated, as without it, the instinct to avoid harm takes control, allows the relationship to deteriorate by withdrawing and adopting a mysterious and reticent demeanor.

BEFORE

77

YOU
GET
MARRIED

Let us now embark on a meaningful conversation about the fundamental inquiries that ought to be pondered upon as a couple before embarking on the journey of matrimony. Although love may serve as the primary impetus behind your choice, it is equally vital to acknowledge the presence of other crucial elements essential for cultivating a harmonious, enduring, and enriching union. Hence, it becomes imperative to engage in profound dialogues encompassing an array of topics, including but not limited to commitment, intimacy, effective communication, collaborative endeavors, and shared values. These discussions, undertaken prior to your wedding ceremony, be it a civil or religious affair, shall lay the foundation for a marriage that flourishes and maintains equilibrium.

Unfortunately, many soon-to-be-married couples often make a crucial error. Upon announcing their engagement, they immediately immerse themselves in the hectic process of planning their wedding day. This involves meticulously selecting top-notch service providers, deciding on the perfect wedding dress or suit designer, touring potential reception venues, dispatching invitations, acquiring wedding rings, and arranging for a stunning bouquet. Undoubtedly, the whirlwind of these activities is undeniably thrilling, and rightfully so.

A successful marriage is not measured by societal standards or material possessions; it is a union where love thrives, and both partners find fulfillment and happiness. It is the ability to navigate through the ebbs and flows of life together, embracing both the joys and sorrows. A successful marriage is a journey of evolution, where two souls intertwine and grow in harmony. Inspiration can be found in both the fictional and real world. Fictional couples often embody the idealistic aspects of love, teaching us valuable lessons about sacrifice, compassion, and resilience. Real-life couples, on the other hand, showcase the beauty of imperfections and the strength that arises from overcoming challenges together. It is in these stories that we find inspiration for our own unique journey. As time passes, marriage faces its share of threats and dangers. The monotony of routine, lack of communication, and the pressures of external factors can strain even the strongest of bonds. However, it is crucial to nurture the flame of love, to continuously invest in the relationship, and to adapt to the changing tides of life. By doing so, couples can overcome these challenges and emerge stronger than ever. Marriage, the ultimate form of commitment, is a choice that goes beyond any other form of union. It is a declaration of love, a promise to stand by each other's side, and a commitment to weather the storms of life together. While other forms of union may offer different benefits, marriage represents a deep-rooted desire for a lifelong connection, a symbol of enduring love.

As a couple, which three values do you prioritize the most (such as faithfulness, mutual assistance, or understanding)? Have your relationship expectations been met thus far? Do you view marriage as merely a practical progression, or do you anticipate significant changes before and after tying the knot? How do you define a successful marriage? Is there a fictional or real-life couple that you and your partner look up to as role models? In your opinion, what are the biggest challenges and risks that marriages face over time? What led you to choose marriage as your preferred form of partnership over other options?

Exploring the depths of sexual intimacy involves unraveling the complex tapestry of sexual fidelity. In this journey, it becomes imperative to establish open lines of communication, allowing for the uninhibited expression of desires, fantasies, and personal boundaries. However, sexual intimacy encompasses more than just the physical act; it delves into the realms of emotional connection and tenderness. By delving into the intricacies of libido levels and contraception methods, couples can navigate their differences together and forge a harmonious bond. At the core of sexual intimacy lies the need for honest and open conversations about one's sexuality. By fostering an environment that encourages dialogue, partners can share their deepest desires, allowing for a deeper understanding of each other's needs and wants. These discussions serve as a foundation for building trust and intimacy, enabling couples to explore new territories together. Libido levels, often varying between partners, can present challenges within a relationship. Addressing these discrepancies openly can lead to finding solutions that satisfy both individuals. Through compromise, creativity, and understanding, couples can discover ways to bridge the gap between their levels of desire, fostering a satisfying and fulfilling sexual connection. Another crucial aspect to consider when discussing sexual fidelity is the compatibility of contraception methods. By evaluating and discussing the effectiveness and convenience of the chosen method, partners can ensure that their sexual experiences are not hindered by concerns about unwanted pregnancies or sexually transmitted infections. This shared responsibility strengthens the bond between partners and enhances the trust within the relationship. Beyond the physicality of sexual intimacy, the role of tenderness and physical touch should not be overlooked. These non-sexual forms of affection are vital in maintaining a deep emotional connection. A gentle touch, an embrace, or simply holding hands can foster feelings of love, security, and intimacy. Assessing the compatibility of the couple's need for physical affection is crucial in creating a well-rounded and fulfilling relationship

Defining sexual fidelity is a crucial aspect of understanding sexual intimacy. It is important to openly discuss and express one's sexuality, including desires, fantasies, and boundaries. It is also essential to address any discrepancies in libido levels and find ways to manage these differences together. Evaluating the compatibility of the contraception method being used is another important consideration. Additionally, beyond the sexual aspect, the role of tenderness and physical touch should be considered and assessed for compatibility within the relationship.

When it comes to relationships, there are countless factors that contribute to their success. From communication and trust to shared values and interests, the list can seem endless. However, one often overlooked aspect that can make or break a partnership is the management of time and finances. In this article, we will explore how couples can find the right balance between togetherness and independence, divide household chores effectively, and navigate the often-tricky terrain of financial management. Time Spent Together vs. Time Spent Separately In any relationship, striking a healthy balance between spending time together and having personal space is crucial. It's important to have open and honest discussions with your partner about your individual needs and expectations regarding personal time. Remember, everyone has different preferences, and finding a compromise that works for both parties is key. Whether it's planning regular date nights or carving out designated alone time, finding a balance that suits your unique dynamic is essential for maintaining a strong and harmonious relationship. Household Chore Management The division of household chores is another area that can greatly impact a relationship. It's essential to establish clear expectations and communication channels to ensure that both partners feel valued and respected. Consider creating a chore chart or schedule that outlines responsibilities and allows for accountability. Additionally, regularly reassessing and adjusting these roles can help prevent resentment or imbalance in the long run. Financial Management: Joint or Separate? When it comes to managing finances as a couple, there is no one-size-fits-all approach. Some couples opt for joint accounts, pooling their resources and sharing financial responsibilities. Others may choose to maintain separate accounts, allowing for individual financial autonomy. And then, there are those who find a middle ground by having both joint and separate accounts. The key is to find a system that works best for you and your partner's unique circumstances and preferences. Contributions to Joint Accounts If you decide to open a joint account, it's important to discuss how you plan to contribute to it. Some couples choose to contribute equally, splitting expenses down the middle. Others may contribute proportionately, based on their individual incomes. Having an open conversation about your financial goals, priorities, and expectations will help establish a fair and sustainable system that works for both of you. Alignment on Financial Philosophy Money can be a sensitive topic in relationships, and differing philosophies about it can lead to conflict. It's crucial to have open and honest conversations about your beliefs, values, and goals regarding money. Are you both savers or spenders? Do you have similar financial priorities? Understanding each other's perspectives and finding common ground can help mitigate potential conflicts and build a solid foundation for a successful financial partnership. Professional Careers and Their Importance Lastly, it's important to gauge the significance of your professional careers in your relationship. Are you aligned in terms of ambition, career goals, and work-life balance? Discussing your aspirations, supporting each other's professional growth, and finding ways to balance career aspirations with personal life can foster a healthy and thriving partnership.

-And until next time, Au revoir!

 In the North Western world love is expressed in different ways and comes at you like a train at full speed. Passionate about writing, James only had scraps of paper on which he started writing again about this beautiful thing called love, in fact, who does not dream of what we call "the perfect life" having a person in whom we can confide, have fun, and indulge with no holding back?

Indeed, his primary concern since this is his 3rd work: is to present poetry as an art accessible to all, that everyone can enjoy reading, so he wrote this book and made sure the texts are simple, rich, easy to relate and read, very revolting, playful, and academic, so that the readers themselves would want to take up their pen in turn to write their own story, ladies and gentlemen here is a story not very long but undoubtedly the aftertaste will last a long time.

And the subject: it is love, one of our serious daily problems